MO-CAR
THE DIARY OF AN ARROL-JOHNSTON DOG CART

by

Marcus Humphrey

To Edward,
I hope you have as much fun with this old girl as I have

Acknowledgements
My thanks go to all those who have helped in the production of this book, in particular Sabine Muir who has handled the printing, Sarah Milford who has kept me right on detail, and my daughter Natasha and son Simon who have kept me up to date on how to use the IT.

MO-CAR - THE DIARY OF AN ARROL-JOHNSTON DOG CART

My name is Mo, I am a double dog cart, and I am No. 261 of a number of cars built by the Mo-Car Syndicate formed between Sir William Arrol and Mr George Johnston in 1898, and which bear the name Arrol-Johnston.

William Arrol was a well-known and successful civil engineer who built the Forth Railway Bridge, and who was responsible for the replacement Tay rail bridge, Tower bridge in London, and the gantry at Harland and Wolff in Belfast, used for building the Titanic and her sister ships.

George Johnston was a son of the Manse, his father being the Minister at West Linton, and he became a brilliant engineer with ideas way before his time. He was a locomotive engineer in Glasgow and is thought to have developed the first British built motor car which was tested on the road in 1895. His opposed piston engine was a remarkable piece of original design and quite unlike any other engine of the period. It was well balanced and relatively efficient although very complicated. The use of pumps for water and oil circulation was very advanced for the time. It worked well and the Arrol-Johnston cars soon gained a reputation for rugged reliability. The Mo-Car Syndicate was incorporated on 30th December 1898 with Sir William Arrol, Archibald Coats, and George Johnston as Directors. The first factory was at Camlachie, but after a disastrous fire there early in 1901, new premises were found at Underwood in Paisley.

Here they began by putting an engine into contemporary vehicles such as a dog cart, which was solid and would sit firmly high up on any road. I was built in October 1902 which is stamped on my cylinder block, and I looked splendid in my varnished oak woodwork, brass fittings and leather upholstery with solid rubber tyres. So splendid that in the spring of 1903 I was bought by a Mr. James Barclay-Harvey of Dinnet for £420, a lot of money but worth every penny! I was taken up to Dinnet via Ballachulish where my first photograph was taken at the Ferry. I know this to be true, as the grandson of the ferryman at that time confirmed it to one of the family who still own me. They could only ferry two cars a day, crossing at slack water as the tide turned, due to the fast tides of up to eight knots. The curtains along the side may have helped to keep the midges off!

The Arrol on the Ballachulish Ferry, 1903

James Charles Barclay-Harvey and his wife Ellen on me at Dinnet, 1904. The Chauffeur Grubb is behind the car to the left.

On arrival at Dinnet I was put into the excellent care of the Chauffer, Grubb, who would start me by pulling the starting rope up over his head and adjust the governor so that my engine ticked over smoothly. Then he would drive me up to the front door of Dinnet House where Mr and Mrs Barclay-Harvey would climb aboard and off we would go for a run down the drive, and sometimes into Aboyne or Ballater. My owner was so pleased with me, that he decided to take me to the South of France in the summer. I was transported to Aberdeen where I was put on a ship for London, and there I was put on another ship this time for Bordeaux. Of course, Grubb travelled with me, and once we reached Bordeaux, he drove me to the Mediterranean coast where we met the Barclay-Harveys, who had travelled there by train. Happily, Mrs Barclay-Harvey kept some notes of the trip which she describes as follows, as published in the 1904 edition of The Car Illustrated Ltd:

"A short account of a Motor Tour on the Riviera this winter may be of interest to some of your readers. Our car, a 12 horsepower Arroll Johnston 6-seater, was sent with the driver by sea from London to Bordeaux, all necessary arrangements for touring in France were made with the Automobile Club Piccadilly. On arrival at Bordeaux, we experienced no difficulty in passing the customs or getting to tour in France, having applied for the necessary driving and circulation permits before leaving London. A start was then made for Toulouse, Montpellier and Hyères, which place makes a good starting point for the Riviera and is also quite worth a visit. With a fast car it can be reached in three days, though the roads are bad all the way, very much cut up & very rough. Both at Toulouse & Montpellier the Hotels are comfortable & if time permits, it is a pity to miss seeing the old Roman ruins at Nimes and Arles & the old "Cité" at Carcassonne all of which you pass through. The Riviera is too well known to require description. The upper Corniche Road from Nice to Menton is well worth the climb giving the finest views along the coast. The road surface is nowhere very good & the extreme pace of French cars & the dust they make necessitate great care in driving. Also,

French carters require so much time to decide which side of the road they will take that it is a wonder accidents are not more frequent.

On passing the Italian frontier just outside Menton a deposit of 112 francs had to be left with the authorities to be refunded on return. The road beyond San Remo winds up and down & in and out along the coast with lovely views of the sea & distant mountains, and it is well worth the journey as far as Spezzia, Allazzio, Nervi or Rapello make good resting places but the road through Genoa for about 8 miles is almost impassable. From Genoa the car can be sent home by sea, or the journey continued to Southern Italy. We retraced our route and intended to return though France by way of Marseilles, Avignon, Lyons, Tours etc but the weather made this impossible, in fact a snowstorm ended our tour, both we and the car having to condescend to the railway. Given good weather, good roads, a good car, a good driver and a good temper we can thoroughly recommend motoring as a good way of seeing the country."

Registration document for the Arrol issued 11 December 1903

Early motor vehicles like myself were considered to be very dangerous, especially to horse drawn traffic, and a man with a red flag had to walk in front of us everywhere we went. As motor vehicles developed into motor cars and became safer with better brakes, this requirement was removed in 1896 when the speed limit was increased from 4 to 12mph.

When I first arrived at Dinnet I didn't have a Number Plate as they hadn't been thought of then, but by December 1903 all motor vehicles had to have one, and on 11th December 1903 I was given the number plate SA3 by Aberdeen County Council, the SA standing for Aberdeenshire. Although I was one of the first motor vehicles in the Shire, SA1 was allocated to South Africa House, and SA2 to a farmer near Turriff.

New Daimler at Dinnet

My happiness at being the family's only motor vehicle did not last long, however, as my first owner wanted something more like a car and with protection from the weather, so he went and bought a Daimler, very flash, and a few years later a Rolls-Royce which was given the nickname "Griselda" by the family! James's son Malcolm took an interest in me and would take me to shooting parties. On one occasion we were returning from a shoot in the Cabrach, quite a distance, when taking a corner in the muddy road we slipped and hit a rock, which broke my front nearside wheel. In those days there were still wheelwrights round almost every corner, so my passengers spent the night locally and the wheel was repaired for us to return home the following day. Another time Malcolm was driving me home from a party when he took a corner too sharply and I went onto my side, tearing the canopy. I cannot remember anything about the Great War as Malcolm was in France and then London until it was over. Being their first car, I was kept by the family, and not disposed of like some of the others.

The old and the new

Griselda, The Vice Regal Car in Adelaide

After Malcolm's election to Parliament in 1923, I was put into a room in the stable block at Dinnet, which had a radiator connected to a stove in Jimmy Sim's flat, and which kept me warm in winter, and there I stayed for many a year. Malcolm was sent to South Australia as Governor in 1939 and took the Rolls-Royce with him, where it became a splendid Vice Regal Limousine which took him to his various duties. When Malcolm came home from Adelaide in 1944, he left the Roller behind, but once back at Dinnet his stepson David took me to pieces but couldn't put me together again!

In 1946 there were a series of Jubilee Cavalcades, in London, Coventry to Birmingham, Manchester, and finally in Edinburgh in October. Photographs of the time show an Arrol-Jonston dogcart playing a leading role.

Jubilee Cavalcade in Manchester, 1946

Jubilee Cavalcade in Edinburgh, October 1946

Jimmy Grant driving the Arrol near Aboyne, 1963

It was nearly another 20 years before Malcolm's grandson Marcus took an interest in me, and asked Jimmy Grant of the Aboyne Filling Station if he would reassemble me. Jimmy had known the car since it first arrived at Dinnet, so he happily took it to his garage in Aboyne, and soon had me running again! This was in 1963 when there was an exhibition at Banchory to commemorate the building at Linwood in Paisley of three famous Scottish cars, the Arrol-Johnston, the Lotus, and the Hillman Imp. Just before the exhibition took place Marcus was driving past the Huntly Arms Hotel in Aboyne and noticed a large collection of smart vintage Bentleys parked outside. I was still at the garage in Aboyne, so Marcus, together with his mother Violet, and Jimmy, started me up and very slowly drove me past the Bentleys to let them and their owners see what a REAL veteran car looked like!! After the Exhibition I was returned to Dinnet until Malcolm died some years later. Happily, he left me to his grandson Marcus who became my third owner and who took a much more lively interest in me.

Violet Humphrey on the Arrol at Banchory; on the left, a Lotus, on the right, a Hillman Imp, 1963

In 1984 Marcus loaned me to the newly created Grampian Transport Museum at Alford, along with a large horse drawn sledge. Here I was well looked after, my woodwork and brasses regularly cleaned, my leather kept soft and of course my engine and all moving parts well oiled. I was one of the star exhibits at the Museum, and was shown to many groups of young children who were longing to climb all over me! My canopy was still at Dinnet however, but in 1984 Marcus had a friend in Aberdeen called George Strathdee who was a veteran car specialist, and he arranged for George to collect the canopy and take it to his workshop, where he repaired it quite beautifully, replaced it on me, and it now looks as good as new. 1984 was important to me in another way, as Marcus was able to buy back the green Mk VII Jaguar which had my Registration number on it! After I stopped being used regularly, Malcolm would put the number SA3 on his current car, so when he bought the Jaguar in 1955 it was transferred on to that. The car was never used after Malcolm's death in 1969, and Marcus bought it from Lady Muriel's executors.

Off to the Museum at Alford with Mike Ward

At the Grampian Transport Museum Alford

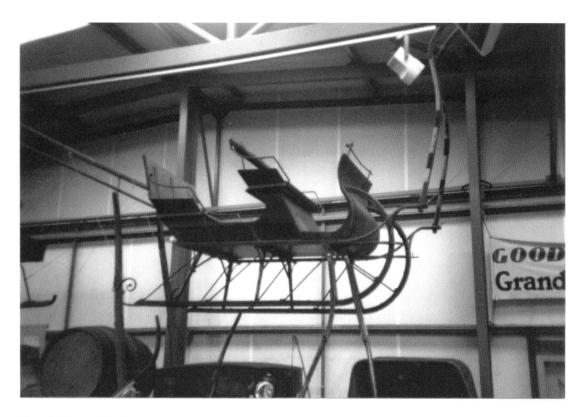

The sledge at the Transport Museum

I was on loan to the Transport Museum each year until the end of 1997 where I continued as one of the principal attractions, albeit a static one, then things began to happen. Marcus' son Edward was due to be married in Aboyne in July 1998 and he thought it would be fun if Edward and his bride were to leave the reception in me! I knew my engine was not in good shape in spite of Jimmy Grant's excellent work, and Marcus found a veteran car specialist called Charles Palmer in Alyth which was not too far away. So, on a cold January day I was taken by covered transporter from the Museum which had become my home, over the hill to Alyth where I was put into the hands of Ian Milford, one of Mr. Palmer's mechanics. Ian and I took to each other right away, he knew instinctively where my weaknesses were and set about repairing them, but it cost Marcus dear, he said Mr. Palmer's invoices made his eyes water! But he knew the work had to be done to get me going properly again, and Ian even had to send to America for a replacement chain drive which luckily were still being made. Other items had to be individually machined by specialist engineers, of which there are a surprising number in the east of Scotland, which helped. Ian and Marcus discussed my water-cooling system and decided it was in working order, which was a mistake as we were to discover on the London to Brighton run some months later!

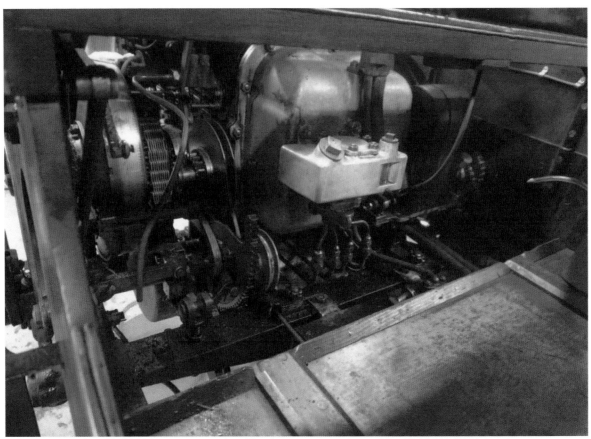

My engine from the front – courtesy of Milford Vintage Engineering

My engine from the back – courtesy of Milford Vintage Engineering

The Date Stamp on the block, 1.10.02 - courtesy of Milford Vintage Engineering

Mr. Palmer was thrilled at having such an important veteran as myself in his workshop as it was good for his business, and word that one of Scotland's first cars was there soon came to the ears of the BBC. After a visit from Euan McIlwraith it was decided that I would be entered for the Brighton run in November and that the BBC would be filming me from start to finish for their Landward series programme which was a lovely boost. Marcus was being encouraged in all this by another Dog Cart owner, Sir William Lithgow, and here I want to give a cautionary tale. Some years ago, Sir William's dog cart was being taken on an uncovered transporter whose driver took a corner a little too quickly, with the result that the dog cart came off and all the original woodwork was destroyed. With most of my weight at the back, it is essential that I am loaded <u>backwards</u> on to trailers in order to keep a proper balance.

How I should be loaded on a trailer - courtesy of Milford Vintage Engineering

Me and friend at Mr Palmer's 1998

The restoration work gradually came together, and Ian had me running very well in the narrow roads around Alyth. My brasses were polished to perfection, the woodwork cleaned, and my leather given special treatment. Marcus decided that it would NOT be a good idea for my big front lamp to run on acetylene again, those lamps were quite dangerous, so he sent it off to a specialist who converted it to electricity, and I now have to carry a small 6-volt battery to make it light up. I was brought back to Dinnet in triumph all ready for the wedding. The Reception was held at the Coo Cathedral at Aboyne Castle in mid July 1998, and Ian himself came up to drive me; it was a beautiful evening, I was decorated with balloons, and all went well for the Bride and Groom, though I only carried them a few hundred yards!

Shortly afterwards I was back at the Alford Museum but only for a day, this time to take part in the Alford Cavalcade. Mike Ward, the Museum Curator, collected me and the canopy the day before on an open transporter. Due to its length the canopy is quite tricky to lift and get right onto its four supporting iron shafts, which requires 3 if not 4 tall, strong men to do it properly, as a slip might tear the canopy again which would be disastrous. On the day Marcus drove me, with Ian's help, around the circuit at Alford much to the crowd's appreciation; Mike said I was the star of the show! Marcus returned the following day and drove me back to Dinnet; it is 19 miles and took just under an hour and three quarters and was wonderful for me to have a really good run again, just like the old days! Then I had to be kept in tip top shape for the London to Brighton run of nearly 60 miles, in three months' time.

Alford Cavalcade 1998. Mike Ward, Marcus and Sabrina, courtesy of Aberdeen Journals Ltd

The London to Brighton Run always takes place on the first Sunday in November, from Hyde Park to Marine Parade in Brighton. The run was originated to celebrate the removal of having a man with a red flag walk in front of a car in 1896, however when the speed limit was raised to 20 mph in 1903 it was decided that no further celebrations were needed. The run was resurrected soon after but there was a cut-off date of only cars built prior to 1st January 1905 being allowed to take part. There are usually around 100 cars from all over the world and for many the long drive is quite a challenge, and some don't make it, but each car is shown at its best and is given lots of TLC from its owner. My owner Marcus made sure that all my brasses were gleaming and the wood and leatherwork in fine condition, and two days before the Run I was collected in a covered transporter and taken down to London. Sir William Lithgow had arranged that Marcus, his wife Sabrina and Ian Milford would stay with his party at the East India Club just off Oxford Street, as the club had secure parking facilities for myself and the other Dog Cart belonging to Sir William. Both groups flew from Scotland to London and anxiously checked us over on arrival.

Fortunately, the day of the run was clear if a little chilly. Marcus and the others were up early, my canopy fitted, oil, fuel and water topped up, and at 6:45am we set off along Oxford Street towards Hyde Park. My side lamps had disappeared at some stage during the War, so Marcus bought a pair of bicycle lamps which he taped onto the lamp holders, as he didn't want to be stopped by the Police for not having lights on a vehicle in the early dawn. But an even bigger worry was if he could get me round Marble Arch safely with all the London buses going much faster than I could! He needn't have worried, however, as London traffic is used to such anomalies, I was treated with great deference, and at my good running speed of 10 miles an hour, made it safely to the starting area in Hyde Park. What a thrill it was to see all the other vehicles assembling and moving into their allotted space, ready for the start, though some were more ready than others!

Marcus being interviewed BBC TV Landward series – BBC Archives

Leaving Hyde Park for Brighton – BBC Archives

Crossing Westminster Bridge on the way to Brighton, 1998

Marcus eventually found the BBC camera crew, who came and did a lot of filming of me, asking Marcus endless questions on how I worked and how it was to drive me. then it was time to get ready to start on the Run itself. In addition to Marcus, Sabrina, Ian, and Charlie Palmer, I had two other passengers, Dudley de Chair and his wife, long-time friends of theirs. Soon we were on our way, across Westminster Bridge, heading for Brighton. But as we made our way through the London suburbs, we had to stop all too frequently for red traffic lights, which of course did not exist when I was young. I became very hot as the water in the radiator was not circulating properly, and eventually Marcus drew me up near a garage so that I could cool down, which took around 45 minutes.

Waiting for my engine to cool down – BBC Archives

The camera crew went ahead, we eventually caught up with them and they did some more filming of me on the open road, before we had to stop again for another cooling off period where water was available. Contestants in the Run were expected to stop over for lunch at Crawley but by the time we got there we were running late so had to give it a miss. We did however meet up with the Lithgow Arrol which was nice. Contestants are allowed around 8 hours to complete the run of 60 miles, as the organisers realise that due to the age of the competing vehicles many will have breakdowns on the way, and those completing the Run within the allotted time receive a medal. As we went past Gatwick Airport, I must have looked incongruous against the modern aircraft!

On our way again - BBC Archives

We were making our way south of Crawley when we came to quite a steep ascent. Ian was driving at this stage, he slowed me right down and said to the passengers "When I say OFF, I mean GET OFF!" to make my load as light as possible. At the right moment he shouted OFF, they all leapt off, he engaged me in first gear, and up the hill I went no problem. Everyone got back on board again and we carried on until we had to make a third cooling off stop. We were a long way from any sign of civilisation, but Marcus' son Edward who was following in the back-up car, saw a cottage near the road and set off to ask for water. There was no reply from the house, but it did have a garden hose which extended just far enough to reach me, the tap was on the outside, and after what seemed an interminable wait, we were off again. By this time, we had only an hour left to get to Brighton, but on open side roads I was able to keep running at my average of 10 miles an hour without overheating, and we pressed on. Soon Brighton itself came into view. The film crew had gone on ahead and thought they would not see us finish, Marcus took over from Ian for the final stretch, and as we tore down a hill into Brighton with only 10 minutes to spare Sabrina's warm woolly hat blew off. "Sorry, I'm not stopping", cried Marcus as my speed reached 25 MPH and soon, we were in sight of the finish on the Madeira Drive, much to my relief and all involved in particular the film crew, who made a big fuss of me, as did Marcus and Ian. My progress in the Brighton Run that year duly appeared on one of the BBC's Landward programmes shortly afterwards and was much appreciated. Marcus was given a copy of the full unexpurgated tape from before the start, to the finish, for his records, as well as a copy of the programme as shown on Landward.

We made it! – BBC Archives

The covered transporter from Auto Services of Perth took me back to Alyth, which gave Ian a chance to completely overhaul my cooling system, which now works beautifully. A new pump was fitted so that my radiator can be filled from a stream or bucket once the engine is running. Having spent so much money on the restoration of my engine and other parts, Marcus took the view that he was going to keep me at Dinnet so that he could take me out for a run from time to time, and use me for family events, rather than have me in the museum, but that he would always take me back there for special occasions, and this is how it was all to turn out.

With Marcus and grandson Harry at Dinnet

With Sabrina and Twiga at Dinnet

On the drive at Dinnet

The following year, 1999, I was taken on an open transporter, carefully loaded backwards, up to Forres in Moray for the Forres Theme Day Association for a celebration of Scottish Cars, where I shared an exhibit with an Albion amongst others. A huge crowd turned out to see all the Scottish built cars, and there was even a jazz band playing! Marcus was given a lovely commemorative crystal goblet with which to remember the event.

At the Scottish Car Exhibition Forres 1999

A nice Albion at Forres

The Tin Pan Alley Band

In July I was back at the Grampian Transport Museum for the annual Alford Cavalcade, Marcus drove across in his British Racing Green MkVII Jaguar having just had the front and rear bumpers re-chromed, so she looked really smart and generated a lot of interest!
The Cavalcade Theme in 2000 was Scottish Built, it was fascinating to see such a variety of Scottish built cars, and to keep me company Mike had loaned an Albion dog cart from the Biggar Trust. Luckily Ian was available to drive me as Marcus was away that day, though he did drive me home a day or two later. Ian drove me in a race against the Albion. We had all of his family on board and Mike had set out two sets of cones on either side of the track. We both lined up on the starting grid and awaited the signal. I was so excited to have someone of my own age to prove myself against! The flag went down and off we flew. Ian's children all hanging tightly onto my lovely brass railings as we sped up the track, weaving in and out of the cones. A swift about turn at the top and we were inching ahead. Back down the track we went with the roar of the crowd encouraging us. In and out, my wheels turning this way and that, could we do it? With Ian's skill and my determination, we won (of course – was it ever in question?)! What a day.

The Mk VII Jaguar

With Ian and family on the circuit at Alford - courtesy of Milford Vintage Engineering

The Ballater Victoria Week Committee contacted Marcus as they wanted a vehicle of (almost) the Victorian era to take part in their Parade through the village in early August. This was agreed to, so Marcus drove me to Ballater with Sabrina to the Monaltrie Park where all vehicles in the Parade were exhibited. To my surprise and delight, I was declared the Best Vehicle in the Parade, so I was chosen to lead the Parade behind the Ballater Pipe Band. Trouble was, the Pipe Band could only move at 4 miles an hour, rather slow for me, and Marcus had to be very careful when engaging my lowest gear, and I got quite hot. All went well however, the crowds cheered, and we had a good run back to Dinnet.

Being looked over before the Ballater Victoria Week Parade

Ready for the Parade with Sabrina, Marcus and Jim Stephen. Best vehicle in Parade!

In 2001 I did the Ballater Parade again, no Pipe Band this time thank goodness, and Marcus decided to take me on the Road Run to Balmoral and back, going out on the South Deeside Road. As we were passing Mains of Abergeldie, my engine lost compression and Marcus just managed to steer me into the yard before I stopped. He could not get me going again but was able to get in touch with Bill Ross of the Dinnet Service Station to come with his trailer and take me back to Dinnet. Ian came to discover the problem and found that I had blown my cylinder head gasket, so he took me back to his workshop and soon had me running again. In 2001 the Cavalcade theme was Grampian Registered, the intention being to gather together as many early motor vehicles as possible that were registered in Grampian with the prefix SA, SU, RG, SO, SE or AV. I certainly qualified, and it was a lovely sunny afternoon.

Later that year, Marcus was at a party at Balmoral and was regaling HM The Queen Mother about the Brighton run, when Her Majesty said to him "Tell me, Marcus, how many steps up into your car?" To which he replied "Two, Ma'am", "Well," came the reply "My father's had three, and I would very much like to see yours." So, a date was arranged in October, Ian was contacted, and he and Marcus both worked on me to ensure that I was in as near perfect condition as possible for this Royal inspection.

Arrival at Birkhall 20 October 2001

With HM the Queen Mother and Marcus

The Queen Mother inspecting me

Leaving Birkhall

The plan was for Marcus and Ian to drive the Arrol from Dinnet to Birkhall, which would probably take around 45 minutes. Unfortunately, the day of 20th October dawned very wet and foggy, so Marcus went to Strachan's in Aboyne where he bought a set of large red bicycle reflectors which he taped to my back, to enable modern cars to see me in the mist and not run into me, as the small paraffin lamp was nowhere near bright enough. We were expected to be at Birkhall at around 2:30pm so set off in good time, and although it was very wet, we had a smooth and uneventful run and soon found ourselves at the front gate to Birkhall. The Metropolitan Bobby opened the gate without question, gave us a salute, and on we went to the front door. As we approached the house, I saw a familiar figure coming down the steps to greet us, Her Majesty herself. We drew up under the covered portico, shut my engine down, and were given a warm welcome by Her Majesty who was fascinated and had a really good look over me, chatting all the time to Marcus and Ian. One of her chauffeurs was also present and in addition to taking a detailed interest, also took some photographs of the occasion. Marcus and Ian were then given a warming stirrup cup which had been prepared for them, such a lovely thought, and after a good half hour or more, it was time to take our leave. Fortunately, the rain had eased off and we had a good run back to Dinnet to round off a magical meeting. The memory of it still brings tears to Marcus' eyes, it was the last time he was to meet this lovely Lady, as she died the following April. He and Sabrina went to Westminster Abbey for her funeral, and I can remember him telling others how appalled he was by the low standard of dress by attending Cabinet Ministers, only the Foreign Secretary's Labrador Guide Dog being properly dressed - in a black tailcoat!

As if that was not enough excitement for a lady rapidly approaching her 100th birthday, my rubber tyres were in a dreadful condition with chunks of rubber coming off. I was taken back to Alyth where Mr. Palmer removed all four of my wheels. They were then taken down to a firm in Kent who look after the Royal Carriages, and who told Marcus "Minimum extrusion £2,000" for the new solid rubber tyres, but well worth it if they will last 100 years as the first rubber did. They did an excellent job in a very short time, and it is almost impossible to see the joints on the tyres. Another addition which Ian picked up from the Lithgow Arrol, was a breather which makes my engine run much more smoothly. My carburettor also had to be completely renovated to help it cope with modern fuels which contain so many additives not available when I was first built. Ian says I am now so well put together that I should last another 100 years, what a wonderful tribute to Scottish engineering!

With my lovely new tyres, the reconditioned radiator, and all the TLC Marcus and Ian had given me, I now felt up to anything, and just as well, as my next adventure was to be an Arrol-Johnston Centenary celebratory run over two days, from Glasgow to Dumfries via Ayr. On 16 May I was transported to the Glasgow Transport Museum, where I met not only Sir William Lithgow's Arrol again, but also TWO other dogcarts, and ten other Arrols built between 1913 and 1924. The other two dogcarts belong to Frank Thomson and Alistair Hacking.

Ready for the off at Glasgow Museum of Transport

The following morning, we were lined up outside the Glasgow Museum of Transport, and at 11am the Lord Provost flagged us off on our way to Paisley. I was really excited at going home, but after 100 years the city had changed enormously and there was very little I could recognise. We formed a parade outside Gilmour Street Station where we were all much admired, then it was a chance to prove ourselves by going up the steep Proving Hill on which I was tested when built, and with Ian at the wheel I made it up again no problem!

Outside Gilmour Street Station, Paisley

Marcus and Ian then took it in turn to drive me to Ayr through lovely countryside, it had been sunny and dry when we left Glasgow, but by the time we reached the Fairfield Hotel some rain had set in. On our way into the town of Ayr, Ian thought it would be prudent to fill my petrol tank for the drive on to Dumfries, so we stopped in an enormous modern filling station. I felt a little self-conscious at being 100 years old, as Marcus and Ian removed the front seat to access my fuel tank, surrounded by modern cars, but no one seemed to think anything about it! My newly conditioned radiator was working well, and I hardly needed any water on the journey over. All 14 of us were parked together in a safe place, though Marcus and Ian did take anything easily removable, such as the horn and my tail-light, into the hotel with them.

At the petrol pumps in Ayr

Outside the Fairfield Hotel in Ayr

After a damp night, we set off on the A713 via Dalmellington to Carsphairn, where we were to have a stop at the Coffee Shop there. It was raining heavily, and either Marcus or Ian took a wrong turning at one point, so we had to go back, and by the time we reached the Coffee Shop they were both cold and wet, and the others had gone on. We caught them up, however, at the St. John's Town of Dalry, where drivers and passengers had a good warming lunch. My fuel, oil and water were all checked, the rain eased off, and we went on our way to Dumfries, arriving at the Cairndale Hotel around 4pm after a much easier run. Ian had been teaching Marcus how to manage my crash gears, especially when changing down, and I could feel he was becoming more confident in doing this. Drivers and guests then spent another convivial evening together in preparation for the final day of the Run.

Lunch stop at Dalry

It was an early start as the drivers had to have us cars on display in Dumfries Town Centre, where we were joined by the Dumfries Classic Car Association and their vehicles which made it a really lovely show which the local people greatly appreciated. With the other Arrol-Johnstons I was then driven to Heathhall where the old Arrol-Johnston factory still stands. It was specially built in 1913 when the move from Paisley took place, was very modern for its time, and was still being used by a firm called Gates who manufactured Wellington boots there. We were all lined up outside the factory for a parade and a photograph, and the drivers were shown around the inside of the building to see the exact areas where the cars were made. Then it was back into town, onto the transporter, and home to Dinnet after a most successful tour.

A good line-up of Arrols in Dumfries

Two Arrol-Johnston 15.9 All Weather Tourers

Off to Heathhall

A good line-up of Dogcarts outside the Arrol-Johnston factory at Heathhall, Dumfries (though they would all have been built in Paisley!)

In July I was taken over to the Grampian Transport Museum for their Silver Jubilee Alford Cavalcade. After a viewing session and a few laps of the track, Marcus then drove me to Castle Forbes, where we were given refreshments. My engine was left idling, and when Marcus met Lord Forbes at the Aboyne Games a few days later, Lord Forbes said too him "Marcus, your car has left an indelible mark outside my front door" to which I think Marcus replied: "You should be so honoured by such a fine lady"! But it reminded Marcus to take oil mats with him in future. Fortunately, a friend of Marcus's, Mark Fleming, had warned him of a very sharp corner on the return route to Alford, which would have come as a surprise even at my low speed, and would most certainly have led to a mishap. Marcus was exceptionally careful, however, and we negotiated the corner safely.

Outside Castle Forbes

My 100th birthday was coming up that autumn, and to celebrate it Marcus was going to take me on the London to Brighton Run again. He had to make the arrangements this time, and the same firm took me down to London in their transporter, though this time I had to be unloaded in Hyde Park and stored overnight in a section of the underground Car Park which Marcus was a little edgy about, as it is so easy for parts to be taken from me. All was well, however, as the security was good, and with Ian's help I started easily and made my way to my allocated place in the starting line-up. This time Marcus and Sabrina had their younger daughter Natasha and younger son Simon on board, but everything went well with no breakdowns, and we were in Brighton, after a good stop for lunch, after only 6 hours driving which was very comfortable.

On the road to Brighton, November 2002

London to Brighton finish at 100 years old!

I was summoned to Alford the following year when the Motorvation theme was The Classic Car Cavalcade. Transported from Dinnet by the faithful George of the 5 Mile Filling Station, there was the usual exhibition in the morning followed by a run, this time up to Craig Castle beyond Kildrummy and Rhynie. Marcus knows the road well, I had been over it when much younger, and with Marcus' skill and patience we made it to Craig Castle in good time for lunch. Coming back to Alford was not so much fun, our route took us along some narrow and twisting roads, and I eventually came to a grinding halt and refused to go any further. Marcus summoned help on his mobile, and I was towed back to Alford, most undignified! Thankfully no damage had been done, I stayed at the Museum for a few days, then on one of the hottest days of the year on 6th August, Marcus drove me home with Edward and Jim Stephen also on board, the run taking only an hour and three quarters for the 19 miles. Marcus complained to Mike Ward about the length of the run to Craig, as I was the only Veteran car, the others were all Classics so better suited to a run of that length, and uphill all the way. In 2004 the Motorvation run was to Cluny Castle, shorter and more level, Marcus had Edward and his son Rory with him, but unlike the previous year it was a cold, dreich day and I don't think young Rory enjoyed it one bit!

At Craig Castle with Jock and Heather Barlas

They didn't think I would make it up the hill!

MOTORVATION:
The Classic Car Cavalcade
Grampian Transport Museum

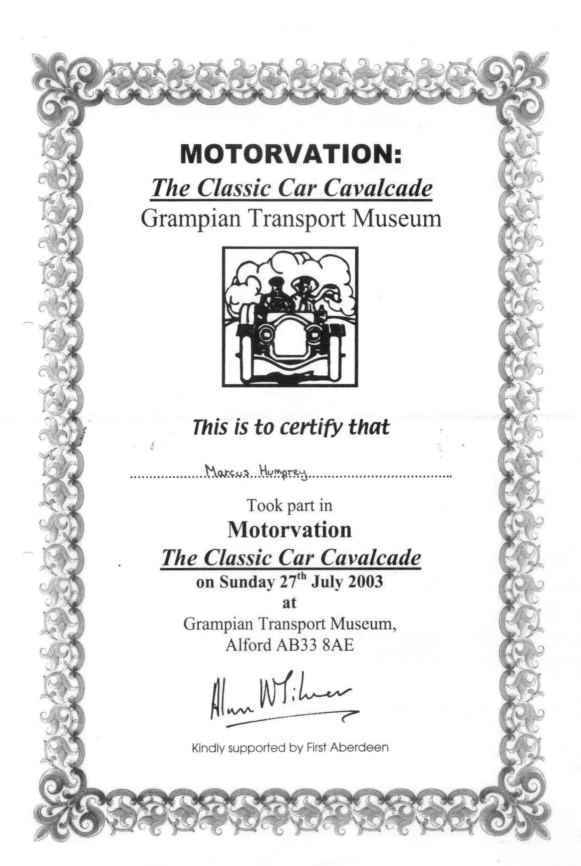

This is to certify that

.... Marcus Humprey ....

Took part in
Motorvation
The Classic Car Cavalcade
on Sunday 27th July 2003
at
Grampian Transport Museum,
Alford AB33 8AE

Kindly supported by First Aberdeen

I had another embarrassing moment on the Run after the Motorvation the following year when, on returning from the flying strip near Insch, I came to a full stop just short of the summit of the Brindie Hill when Marcus had Harry and Lemina Lawson-Johnston as passengers. Happily, I was towed to the top of the hill, given a good push, Marcus got me going again and I made it safely to Alford.

Harry and Lemina at Brindie Hill

Mike Ward looked after me there until 16 September, when I was transported down to West Lothian where I met Marcus and many other Arrol-Johnston cars the next day. The 17th September was the 150th anniversary of the birth of George Johnston, the co-founder of the Mo-Car syndicate, we drove to the Manse in West Linton where he was born, and where a blue plaque was attached in his memory. Although rather wet, it was a happy day and good to see more vehicles of my marque.

2006 saw Ian and his wife and four girls back on board again for the Motorvation run. We set off from the museum and I was going like a train! I took the long downhill straight towards Monymusk with ease and the children squealed with delight as my speed got up into the 20s! After a delicious lunch stop at Monymusk house, and lots of admiration from fellow classics, we set off on a different route home. Well, all that downhill meant that I had to go UPHILL for the return! As the roads got steeper, I slowed down more and more. Eventually, on one very long, steep hill I almost ground to a halt, so Ian once again instructed his passengers to dismount and the girls all trudged slowly up the hill behind me. Help was at hand for Ian's wife and their 7- year-old when a young whippersnapper of an Austin 7 stopped to give them a lift. The other 3 girls walked on to the top of the hill and jumped back on board for me to limp back to the museum. Ian realised that I needed a trip to his lovely new workshop in Kirkmichael and I headed off their soon after.

Outside the Manse at West Linton

Plaque to George Johnston at West Linton

With Marcus at West Linton 2005

More modern Arrols at West Linton

For the next 10 years I was a regular attraction at Alford for the Cavalcade or Motorvation, often doing the run including one to Lumsden with Richard Marsh, and another to Castle Forbes. In 2009 I won the prize for "Best Made in Scotland" which was most gratifying. Sometimes Marcus was not able to drive me himself, so Ian would come and help out, as those two were the only people who knew how to drive me and were insured to do it! I was also a regular in the Ballater Victoria Week exhibition and parade, and in 2011 was awarded the Michael Sheridan Trophy for Best Car. Marcus was so thrilled that we did the Crathie run again, with Brian Smith and his son Angus as passengers. A few years beforehand I had taken a lady dressed as Queen Victoria around the village in pouring rain! In late July it was his brother-in-law Michael Pooley's 70th birthday. All the family were at Dinnet and I was very happy to take them for rides up and down the Drive. Marcus usually tries to get Edward to come with him on journeys such as returning from Alford, so that he can teach him how to drive me.

'Queen Victoria' in Ballater Victoria Week Parade – photo courtesy of Alistair Cassie

Alford Cavalcade with Irek, Castle Forbes 2007

Ballater Victoria Week Parade – photo courtesy of Alistair Cassie

Changing gear with crash gears in a leather lined clutch requires no little amount of skill as Marcus himself has found out! He has only recently come anywhere near perfection, and the driver has to remember that I am the boss, not him, and if it means stopping and moving off again, so be it. After all, my average speed is only 10 mph, less than a bicycle! On the main roads, most modern cars, their drivers and passengers are usually amazed to see such a historic vehicle actually moving and give me plenty of room, but the odd driver gets a little impatient, some cutting in too early after overtaking, not realising I only have shoe brakes. In July Edward and Marcus had a lovely training drive home from Alford, making it back to Dinnet just before a thunderstorm broke!

At Alford with Marcus and Edward 2007

In 2005 Ian set up on his own at The Garage in Kirkmichael, and he took me there the following year as my pistons were needing re-ringed amongst other things. He went over me very thoroughly again, taking me out for test drives, and I soon became a familiar sight around the village. The re-ringing of the pistons has greatly increased the compression and makes it much more difficult to start on the rope, even when my engine is warm, as Marcus was soon to discover. A tow-start however usually gets me going without much difficulty, and the new water pump takes up water very quickly from a bucket.

Ian and technician checking my engine - courtesy of Milford Vintage Engineering

Refreshment time! - courtesy of Milford Vintage Engineering

With Marcus and Twiga at Ballater 2009

With Lynton Black at Ballater 2009

As Winner of the Michael Sheridan Trophy 2011

2012 was the year of Her Majesty the Queen's Diamond Jubilee, and all up and down Great Britain and throughout the Commonwealth, preparations were in hand to celebrate it in an amazing variety of ways. In Ballater it was decided, amongst other things, to elect two schoolchildren to be King and Queen of Ballater for the day, and I was asked to drive them through the village as they would be so easily seen. Marcus had me "Dressed overall" with miniature Union flags attached around my canopy and I looked very smart as he drove me up to Ballater to receive Their Majesties. Happily, it turned out to be a lovely summer's day, crowds had gathered in the village and cheered as the Royal couple passed by, waving in traditional style. This was followed by a Street Party on the Green, and great fun was had by all. Marcus had driven me up to Ballater in 45 minutes, and home again in 31, as it is downhill all the way, reaching a top speed of 25mph(41kph) going down into the Mossy Haugh west of Dinnet.

Dressed Overall for the Diamond Jubilee

The King and Queen for the day arrive at Ballater's Street Party

The Grampian Transport Museum Curator, Mike Ward, knows my importance in teaching children about the transition from horse drawn carriage, through horseless carriage, to motor vehicle, and was desperate to have me back at Alford on display, so in 2015 Marcus agreed to let him have me as long as he could take me out for a special event, which was agreed. I had hardly been installed at the Museum when Mike rang Marcus to say that a Mr Paul Atterbury was interested in me, and would he come over and speak to him. Mr. Atterbury is one of the specialists on the Antiques Roadshow (a television programme where people bring their treasured articles for appraisal), and was so fascinated by me that, even though the Roadshow does not normally look at cars, he wanted me to come to Balmoral when they would be filming there at the end of July. Invitations were also issued to Sabrina, Edward and Tania. Mike agreed to my absence for a while, as long as Marcus mentioned "Grampian Transport Museum" somehow, and George was booked to take me there and back to Dinnet. We had been asked to be at Balmoral by 8:30am but Marcus explained that we could be a little late, as George had to collect the canopy on his way past Dinnet which would slow things down.

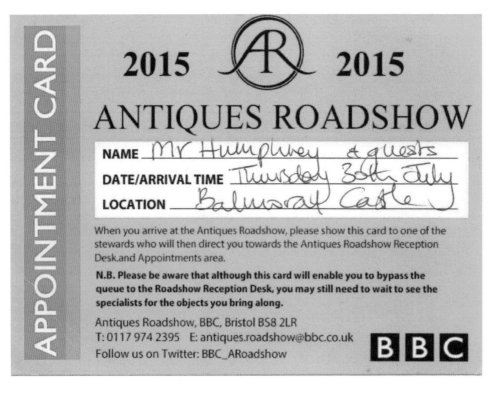

Marcus' invitation to take me to the Roadshow

The day arrived clear and sunny but with a cold wind for that time of year. George was allowed to take me right up to the Stables Yard at Balmoral where I was unloaded, then Marcus realised he did not have enough tall men to help put my canopy on. Wondering what to do, he was surprised when a group of soldiers on the Royal Guard appeared as if by magic and said: "Can we help?" The canopy was on in no time, then Marcus tried to start me, but the journey and cold morning had unsettled me, and I was unwilling to fire up. Eventually I was towed gently around the stable block, Marcus let in the clutch ever so gently, and off I went with a BANG and a BUCK, losing my tail lamp in the process, which was happily returned to Marcus by one of the staff.

By this time, it was nearly 9:30 and queues were forming on the lawn in front of Balmoral Castle. Marcus drove me around to the front, where he was amazed to see Sabrina about to be filmed with a tiara! Edward was also about to be filmed with his piece of Lalique glass which Marcus had rescued from being thrown into a skip! I suddenly became the centre of attraction for a film crew, who asked Marcus to drive me backwards and forwards across the front of the Castle and toot the horn, until another crew called out "Stop that tooting, we're trying to film!" I was filmed from every possible angle, Marcus asked every possible question about me and yes, he did mention Grampian Transport Museum in one of his replies! By 11am they had done enough, Marcus drove me back to the Stable Yard where George was waiting to take me back to Dinnet, to be there for the Ballater Victoria Week Parade in 10 days' time. Unfortunately, the presenter, Fiona Bruce, did not arrive until lunchtime, so I was unable to give her a ride. The crews filmed enough for two shows which went out in December that year, with Sabrina appearing in the first, and Marcus and Edward in the second; I was certainly noticed.

Me and Marcus being filmed at the Antiques Roadshow at Balmoral Castle 2015. BBC Archives

Edward being interviewed for the Antiques Roadshow at Balmoral. BBC Archives

The Parade in Ballater was another great success on a glorious sunny day, and a fortnight later I was giving rides up and down the drive at Dinnet to guests at Marcus' younger son Simon and his bride Caroline's wedding party. I have had a truly lovely time with the family and am now well known locally, as Marcus occasionally takes me out for a run to Aboyne and back to get petrol, or just for the fun of it! The fact that I am still in good running order at the age of 120 is much appreciated. In 2015 however Marcus decided it was time to hand on ownership to his elder son Edward, especially as Marcus and Sabrina now live in Aboyne and cannot give me the close attention I sometimes need. Being a running motor vehicle Marcus did not have to pay Capital Gains Tax on the transfer, but my number plate of SA3 was considered to be a separate item with its own value, and CGT had to be paid on that, much to M's displeasure! Edward now takes great care of me, and in winter sets traps for mice who otherwise would chew my leathers, especially the covers, and have even been known to chew the handle of the starting rope.

with Edward, the fourth generation of the family to own me

Two years later, Mike Ward was in touch with Marcus, as he had been asked to source an early car in running order for a new TV series, Great British Car Journeys, part of which was to be filmed at Culloden near Inverness by Tern TV. Edward agreed to make me available, Marcus would drive it on behalf of GTM, and his neighbour Philip Cruickshank had a covered transporter to take me to the Culloden House Hotel where the filming was to take place. I was taken up on a lovely day in late June, we found the Hotel with no difficulty, and I was unloaded to await the arrival of the film crew with the two TV personalities who were to take part. On arrival the film crew seemed to take forever to get set up, with microphones and cameras here, there, and everywhere including a tiny camera clipped to the rim of the canopy. At first Marcus did not recognise the two TV personalities so was not in awe of them, but eventually the penny dropped as they were Peter Davison and Christopher Timothy, leading lights from the very well-known series All Creatures Great and Small. When the moment came, I started easily, ran well, and everyone was very impressed, with the filming completed in just over 10 minutes! I was in the first programme when the series finally went out in January 2019, and it was rebroadcast in the autumn; some of Marcus' friends recognised him.

Filming for Great British Car Journeys TV series 2019 – Courtesy of Tern TV

2019 saw the opening of the Aberdeen Western Peripheral Route (AWPR) which had been under construction for many years, and which it is hoped will ease the flow of traffic in and around Aberdeen. A static display of vehicles of all ages was mounted near the crossing over the Dee, and Mike Ward arranged for me to be taken to it, to show the public just how much car design has changed over the last 120 years! The new road is lovely, wide, and with easy gradients; I was longing to be taken for a drive on it, but sadly that was not allowed.

The static display on the Aberdeen Western Peripheral Route

Last year, 2020, has seen another unusual twist to the Arrol-Johnston story. In 1905 the Egyptian Government had purchased one of the last dog carts to be built, and it was used by their army to draw and power a spotlight but has lain in a museum in Khartoum for over 100 years without any attention. The Sudanese Government, more appreciative than most of their colonial connections, have asked the British Council to find out how to conserve this Arrol, and their representative Michael Mallinson made contact with Ian Milford who promptly got in touch with Marcus. Mr. Mallinson recently came to Dinnet to film me very comprehensively with Ian pointing out and describing all my parts in the greatest detail, and Marcus has given them the surplus rubber tyre left over when mine were renewed. Marcus was also interviewed about my history for a video which will be placed beside the Khartoum Arrol at the Museum, with subtitles in Arabic! What was particularly interesting to Marcus is the connection with his great-great uncle George Harvey Pasha who was Chief of Cairo City Police in 1914.

The 1905 Arrol Dogcart in the Khartoum Museum – courtesy of Sudan National Corporation for Antiquities and Museums

I cannot conclude this story without mentioning one or two other Arrol-Johnston cars. Perhaps the most famous is the one which Shackleton took on his 1907 tour of Antarctica in Nimrod. It had runners on the front wheels and knobs on the rear wheels, which it was hoped would speed the journey to the South Pole, but the Antarctic snow was too soft, it sank into it so could not be used. The car was put back aboard Nimrod where it was lashed to the deck, but in a heavy storm the ties broke, and the car plunged to the bottom of the ocean, never to be seen again, a sad ending to a hopeful challenge.

Arrol-Johnston on sea ice near Cape Royds

The Arrol modified for Antarctic snow

Marcus says that when he and Sabrina were in New Zealand in 2005, he saw two Arrol cars of 1911 and 1912 vintage, but his greatest thrill was being taken for a drive in a 1929 Arrol in Christchurch which was being lovingly maintained by a Masonic friend of his.

1929 Arrol-Johnston in Christchurch, New Zealand

Since my engine was reconditioned 24 years ago, I have had a much more exciting life, which I hope will continue under Edward's ownership, and that of many generations of the family to come. I believe that I am the only dogcart with its original canopy, and I am proud to continue running as an important contribution to Scottish motoring history.

Some of my trophies

Printed in Great Britain
by Amazon